BOOK • VIDEO

HOT LICKS

JAMES BURTON

THE LEGENDARY GUITAR

ISBN: 978-1-5400-2503-6

HAL•LEONARD®

Visit Hal Leonard Online at
www.halleonard.com

Contact Us:
Hal Leonard
7777 West Bluemound Road
Milwaukee, WI 53213
Email: info@halleonard.com

In Europe contact:
Hal Leonard Europe Limited
42 Wigmore Street
Marylebone, London, W1U 2RN
Email: info@halleonardeurope.com

In Australia contact:
Hal Leonard Australia Pty. Ltd.
4 Lentara Court
Cheltenham, Victoria, 3192 Australia
Email: info@halleonard.com.au

CONTENTS

BIOGRAPHY

Guitarist James Burton was born August 21, 1939 in Louisiana, where he grew up listening to early influences like Bo Diddley, Chet Atkins, and Chuck Berry on the radio.

His music career began at age 14, when he was offered a job as the guitarist on the famed 1950s radio show *Louisiana Hayride.* It was on this show that Burton gained a love of steel guitar from *Hayride* steel guitarist Sonny Trammell.

After a year-long stint with the *Hayride*, Burton joined Dale Hawkins's band, which was signed by Chess Records in 1955. Burton wrote the music for the 1957 Hawkins hit "Susie-Q," which also featured Burton on guitar. He then joined James Kirkland and Bob Luman and recorded a few hits, including "My Gal Is Red Hot" and "A Red Cadillac and a Black Mustache."

Burton next moved to Hollywood, where he joined Ricky Nelson's band and recorded smash hits like "Hello Mary Lou" and "Travelin' Man." During this stint (1958–1964), he also appeared regularly on the popular television show *The Adventures of Ozzie and Harriet.* By the time Burton left Nelson's band, he had already invented his unique "chicken pickin'" technique, for which he employed a normal flat pick with his thumb and index finger in combination with a fingerpick on his middle finger.

In the years that followed, Burton played with various artists including the Monkees, Buffalo Springfield, Joni Mitchell, Judy Collins, Willie Nelson, Frank Sinatra, Dean Martin, Jerry Lee Lewis, Roy Orbison, and Johnny Cash, among others. Burton also joined Merle Haggard and Buck Owens to help create the famous "Bakersfield sound."

In 1968, Burton was nominated for a Country Music Award for "Best Lead Guitar"—and was nominated an addition seven times over the following decade before finally winning.

In 1969, Burton began to tour, record, and perform regularly in Las Vegas with Elvis Presley. He played with "The King" from 1969 until Presley's death in 1977. During this same time period, Burton recorded and toured with Emmylou Harris, who reportedly scheduled her tours around Elvis's schedule just so she could have Burton on board.

Following Presley's passing, Burton played with John Denver for over a decade. In 1986, he teamed up with Elvis Costello to record a total of four albums.

With all his credits as a sideman and a career that spans six decades, Burton has only recorded two solo albums: his 1969 release *Corn Pickin' and Slick Slidin'*, which he recorded with pedal steel guitarist Ralph Mooney; and 1971's *The Guitar Sounds of James Burton*.

In 2001, Burton was inducted into the Rock and Roll Hall of Fame. He has also been recognized by the Rockabilly Hall of Fame, the Musicians Hall of Fame and Museum, and the Louisiana Music Hall of Fame.

In 2009, Burton won a Grammy Award for Best Country Instrumental Performance, along with country guitar legends Vince Gill, Steve Wariner, Redd Volkaert, Albert Lee, John Jorgenson, and Brent Mason, for his playing on Brad Paisley's barn-burning country guitar number "Cluster Pluck."

DISCOGRAPHY & SUGGESTED LISTENING

SELECTED DISCOGRAPHY

James Burton
Corn Pickin' and Slick Slidin' (See for Miles, 1969)
The Guitar Sounds of James Burton (A&M, 1971)

Dale Hawkins
Fool's Paradise (Beveric, 2000)

Rick Nelson
Songs by Ricky (Imperial, 1959)
Ricky Sings Again (Imperial, 1959)
More Songs by Ricky (Imperial, 1960)
Rick Is 21 (Imperial, 1961)
Album Seven by Rick (Imperial, 1962)
Rick Nelson Sings for You (Decca, 1963)

Elvis Presley
On Stage: February 1970 (RCA, 1970)
Elvis in Person at the International Hotel: Las Vegas, Nevada (RCA Victor, 1970)
Elvis [1973] (RCA Victor, 1973)
Recorded Live on Stage in Memphis (RCA, 1974)

SUGGESTED LISTENING

Chet Atkins
Chet Atkins' Gallopin' Guitar (RCA Victor, 1952)
Stringin' Along (RCA Victor, 1953)

Chuck Berry
Rockin' at the Hops (Chess 1960/Chess/MCA 1987)
St. Louis to Liverpool (Chess, 1964)

Bo Diddley
Bo Diddley (Chess, 1958)
Go Bo Diddley (Chess, 1959)

Rick Nelson
Ricky Sings Again (Imperial, 1959)
More Songs by Ricky (Imperial, 1960)

Elvis Presley
Elvis [1973] (RCA Victor, 1973)
Recorded Live on Stage in Memphis (RCA, 1974)

James Burton
Corn Pickin' and Slick Slidin' (See for Miles, 1969)
The Guitar Sounds of James Burton (A&M, 1971)

Chapter 1: Hybrid Picking Technique

Example 1
(:16)

*P.M. refers to downstemmed notes only.

Example 2
(1:50)

**T = Thumb on 6th string

Chapter 2: Steel Guitar Licks

Example 3
(:29)

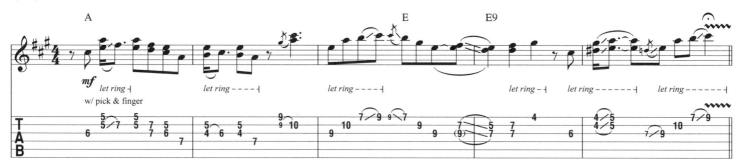

Example 4
(:55)

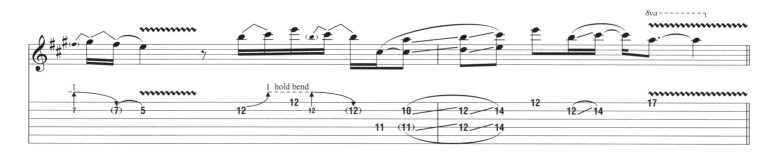

Example 5
(1:16)

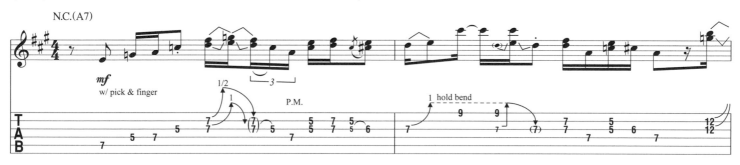

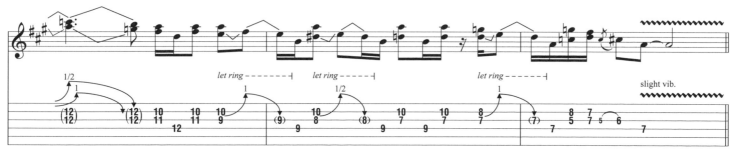

Chapter 3: "Echo Effect" Rhythm Technique

Example 6
(1:12)

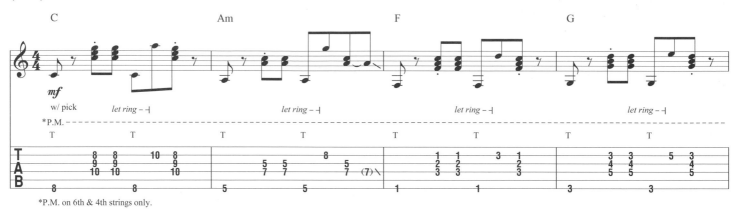

*P.M. on 6th & 4th strings only.

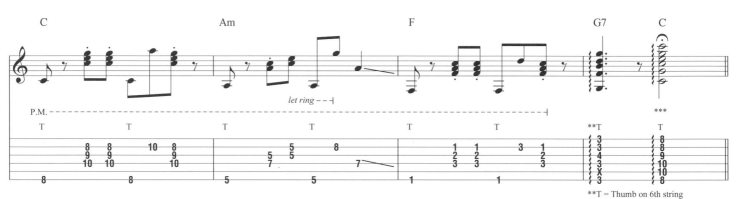

**T = Thumb on 6th string

***Ring-finger barres
10th fret A & D strings.

Example 7
(1:52)

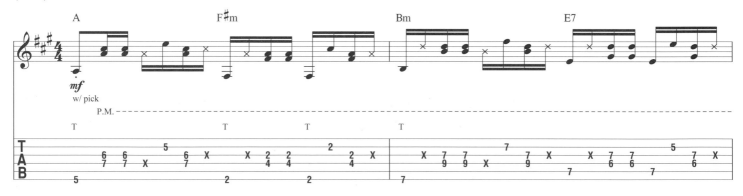

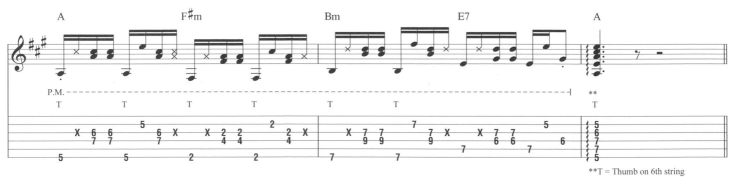

**T = Thumb on 6th string

Example 8
(2:15)

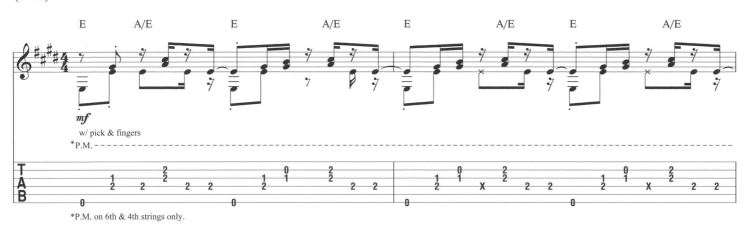

*P.M. on 6th & 4th strings only.

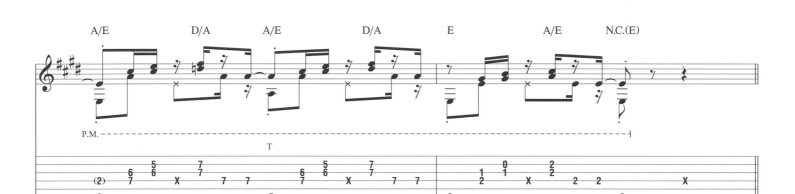

Example 9
(2:35)

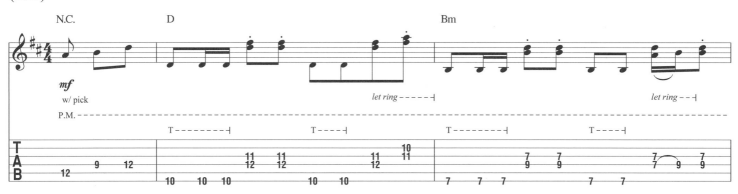

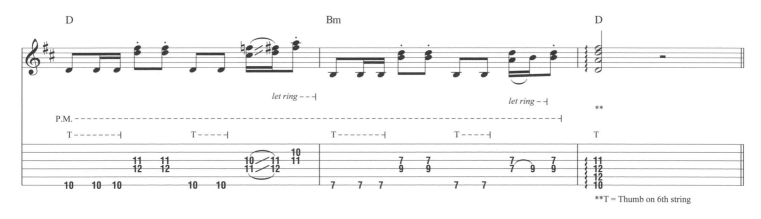

**T = Thumb on 6th string

Chapter 4: Solos

Example 10
(1:19)

*P.M. on 5th & 6th strings only.

**Partial slide.

Example 11
(2:32)

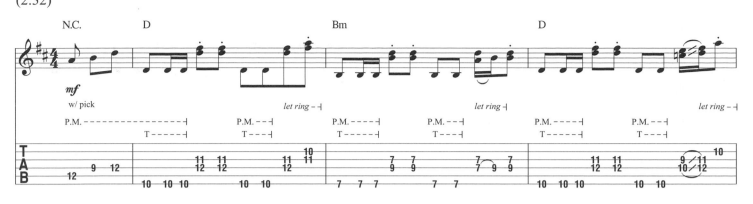

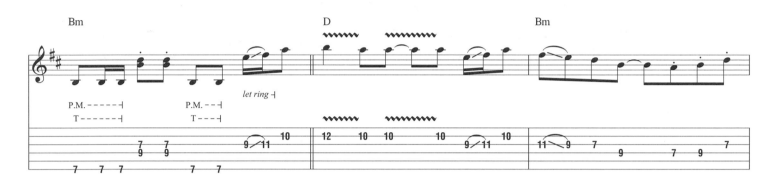

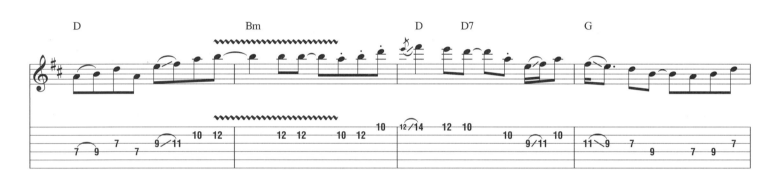

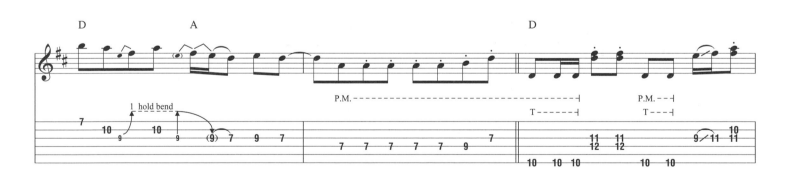

*T = Thumb on 6th string

Example 12

(3:25)

*P.M. & T on 6th string only.

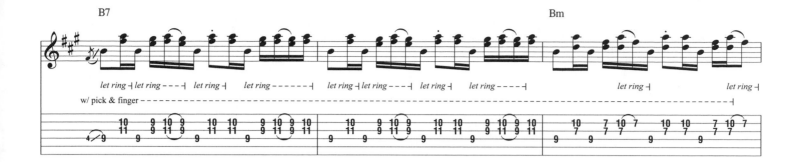

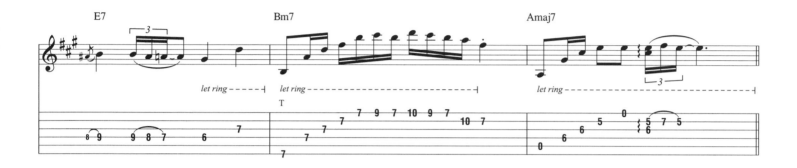

Chapter 5: Chicken Pickin' and Country Bends

Example 13
(:36)

Example 14
(1:09)

Example 15
(1:22)

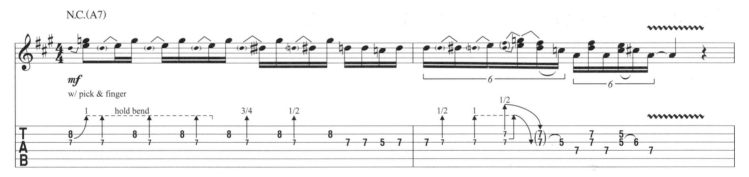

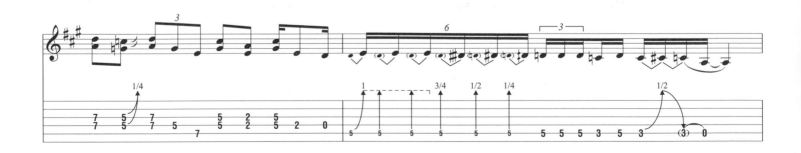

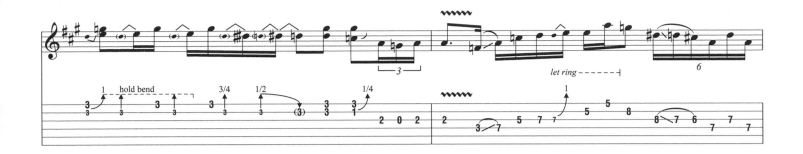

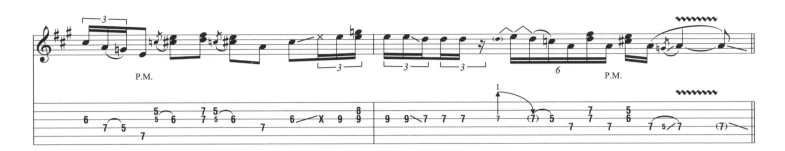

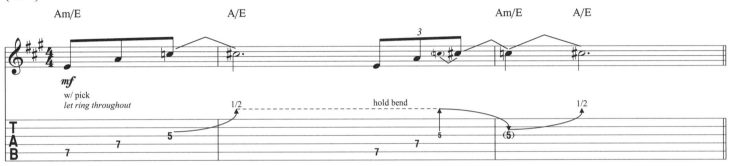

Example 16: Half Note Bend
(2:04)

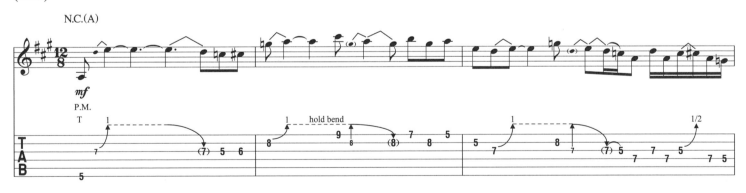

Example 17
(2:21)

Example 18: Country Bend
(2:45)

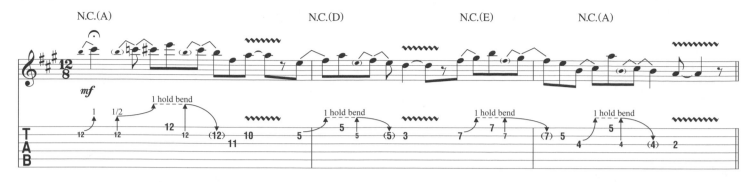

Example 19: Blues Bend
(3:09)

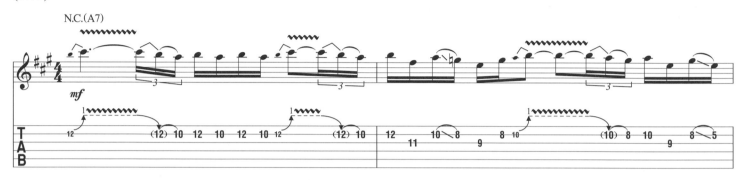

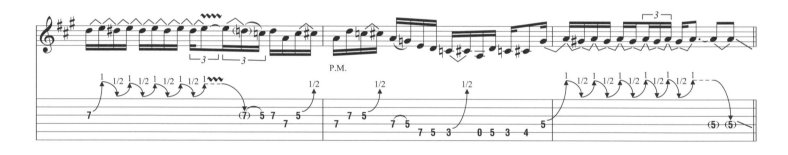

Example 20
(3:36)

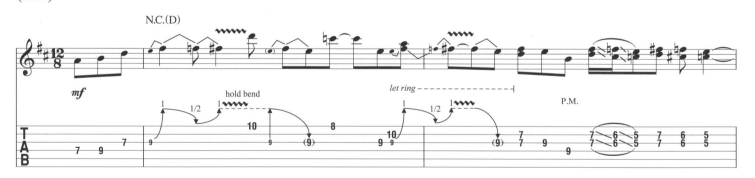

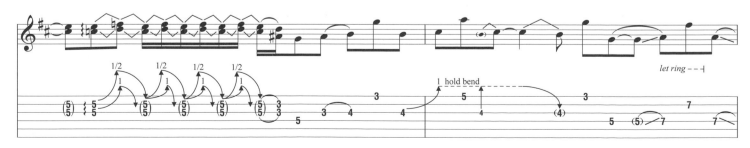

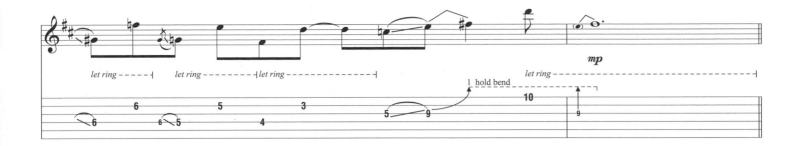

Chapter 6: Behind the Nut & Harmonics

Example 21
(:29)

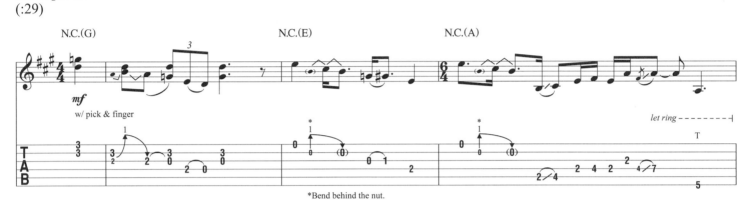

*Bend behind the nut.

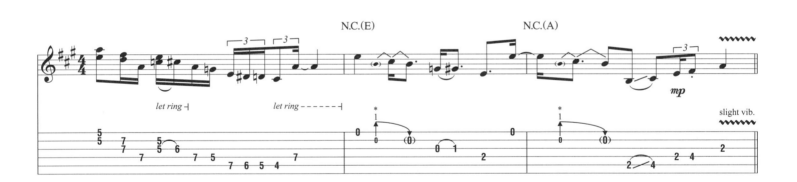

Example 22
(1:00)

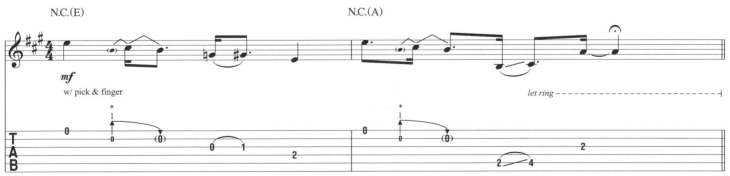

*Bend behind the nut.

Example 23
(1:18)

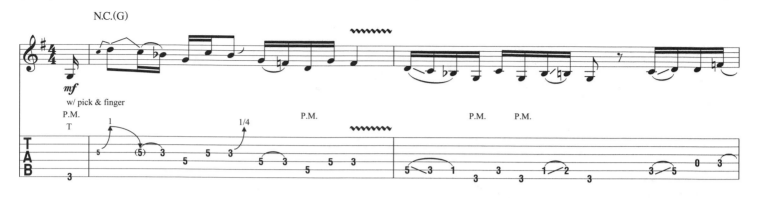

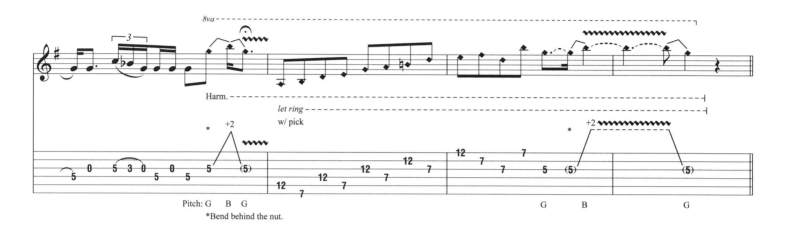

Example 24
(1:50)

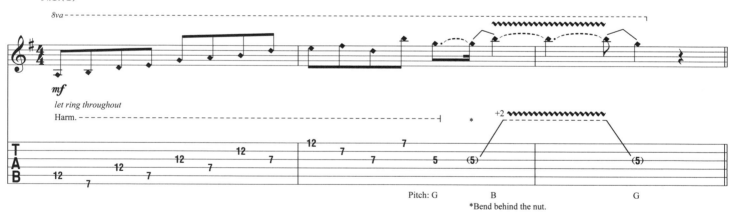

Example 25
(2:00)

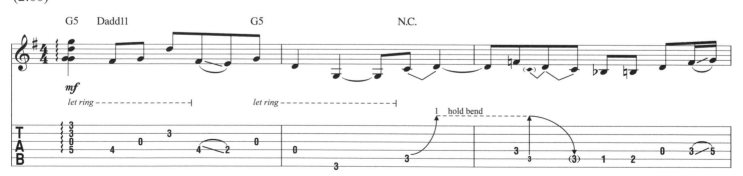

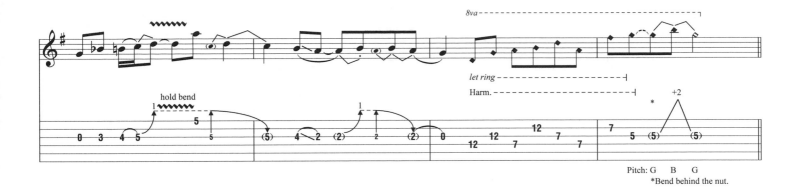

Pitch: G   B   G

*Bend behind the nut.

Chapter 7: String Bending & Drop D

Example 26
(:18)

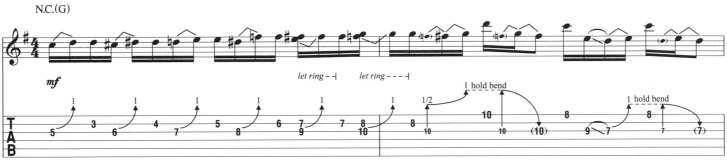

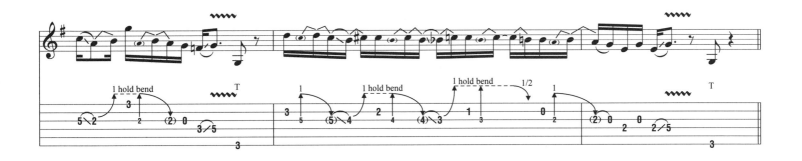

Example 27: Bending Down
(1:23)

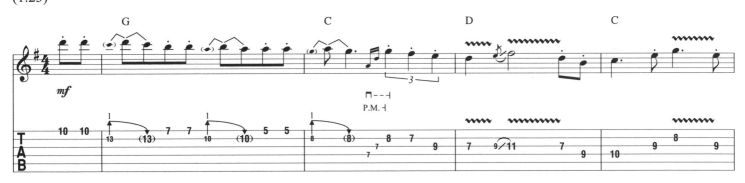

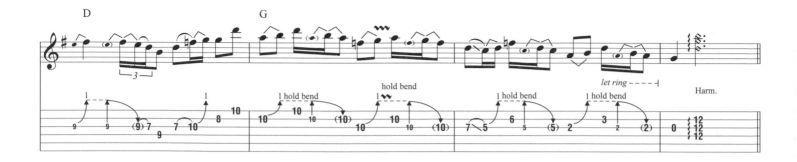

Example 28

(3:00)

Drop D tuning,:
(low to high) D-A-D-G-B-E

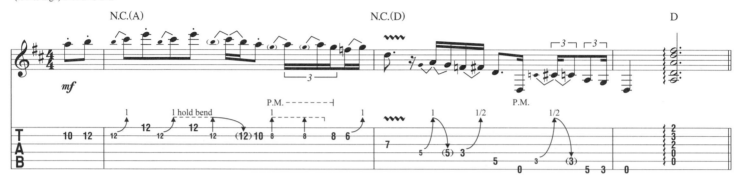

Example 29

(3:32)

Drop D tuning,:
(low to high) D-A-D-G-B-E

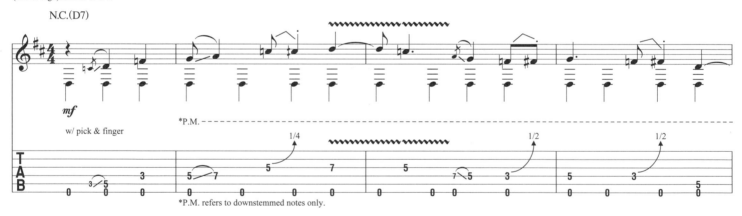

*P.M. refers to downstemmed notes only.

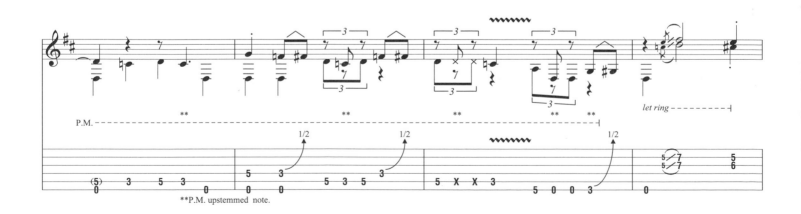

**P.M. upstemmed note.

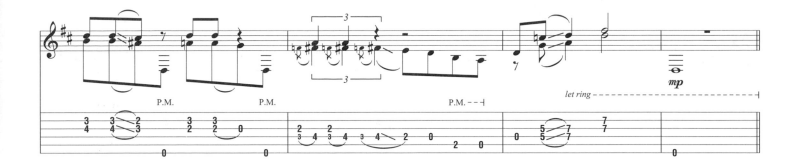

Example 30: Tuning Peg
(4:06)

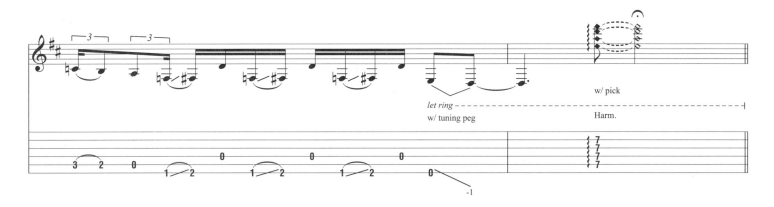

Example 31
(4:45)

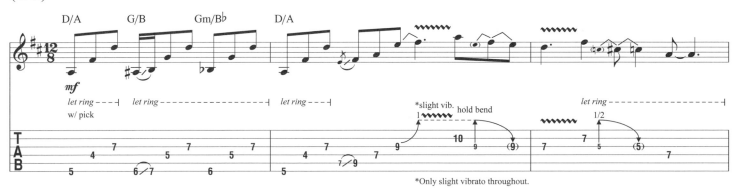

*Only slight vibrato throughout.

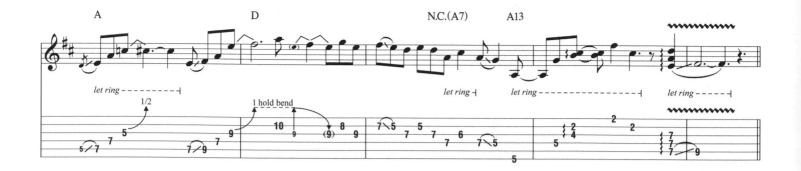

Example 32
(6:42)

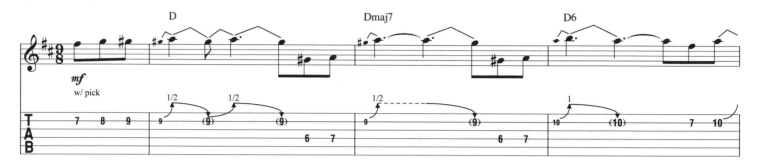

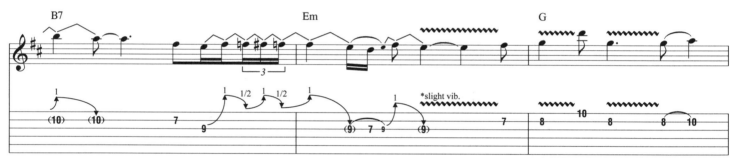

*Only slight vibrato throughout.

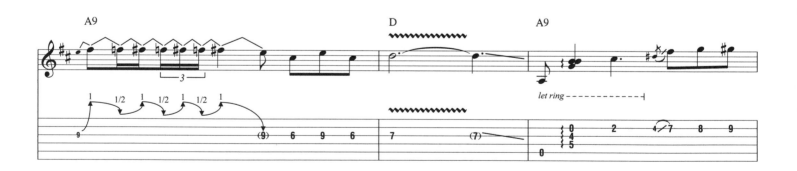

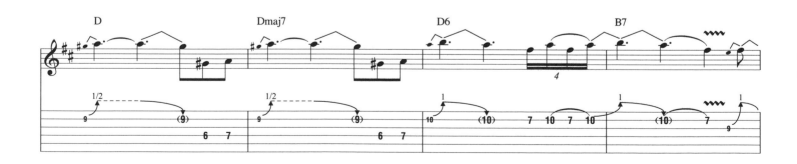

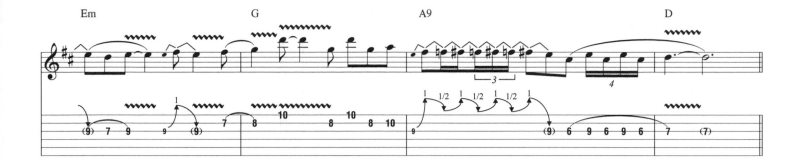

Chapter 8: Cross-String Picking and Licks in E

Example 33
(:35)

Example 34
(1:22)

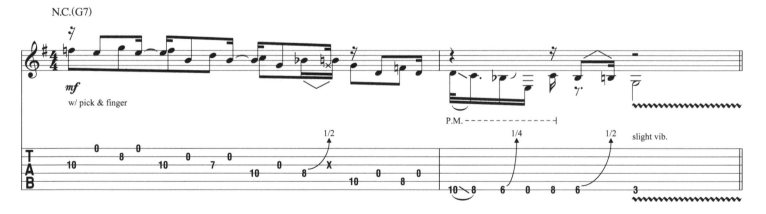

Example 35
(1:53)

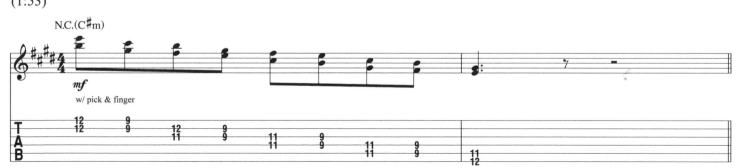

Example 36
(2:08)

Example 37: Rhythm Pickup
(2:31)

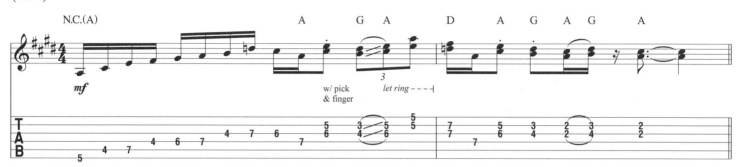

Example 38: Out-of-Phase Sound
(2:40)

Example 39: Middle Pickup
(2:58)

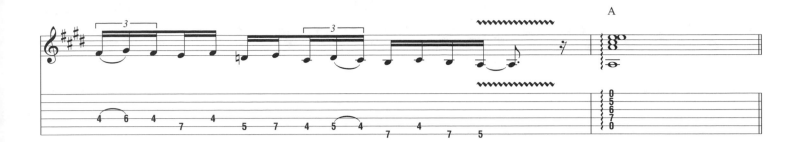

Example 40: Out-of-Phase Lead Pick-Up
(3:13)

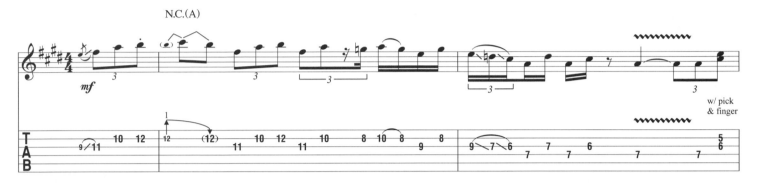

Example 41: Lead Pickup
(3:28)

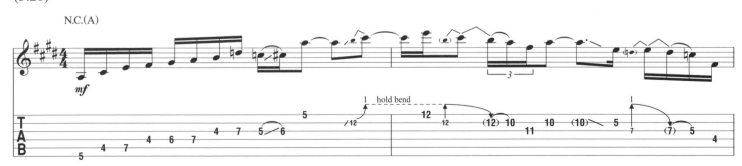

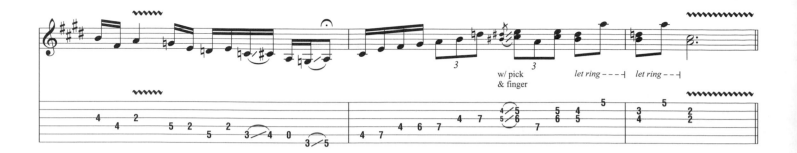

Chapter 9: Elvis Sounds

Example 42
(:25)

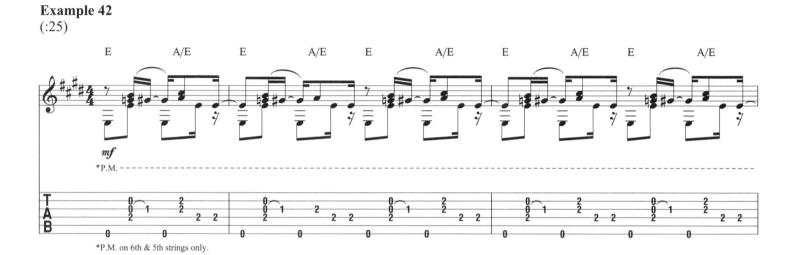

*P.M. on 6th & 5th strings only.

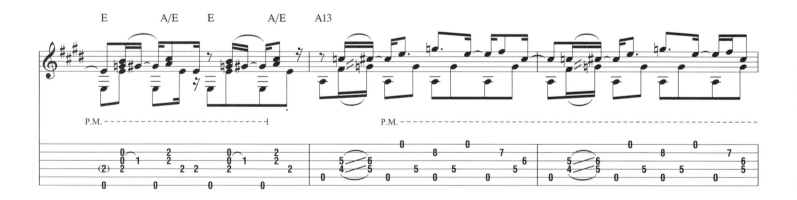

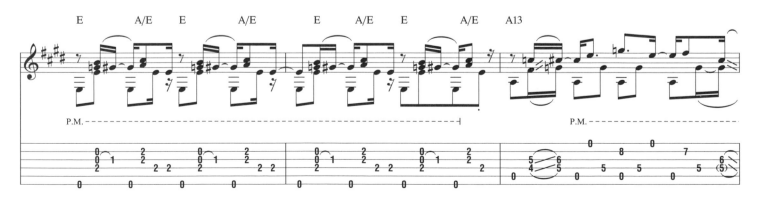

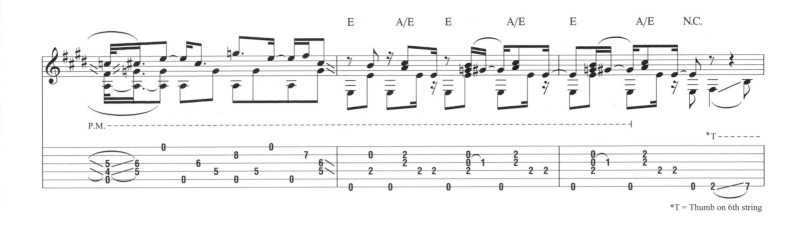

*T = Thumb on 6th string

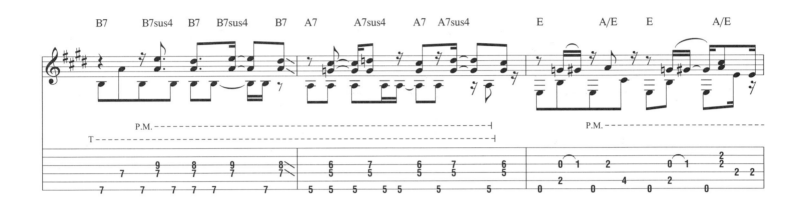

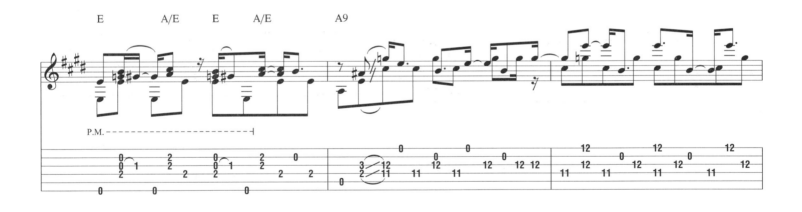

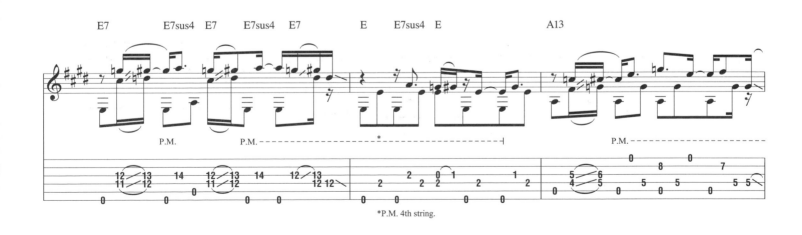

*P.M. 4th string.

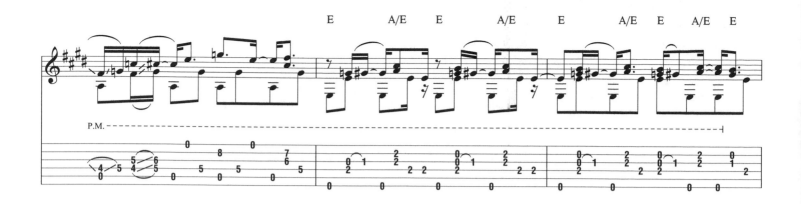

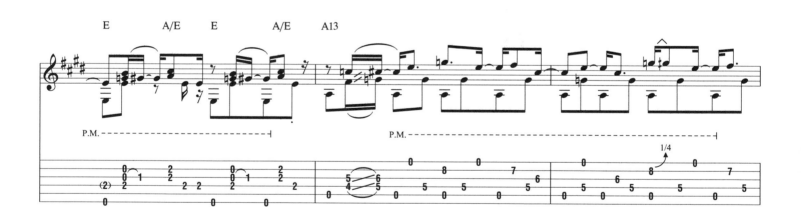

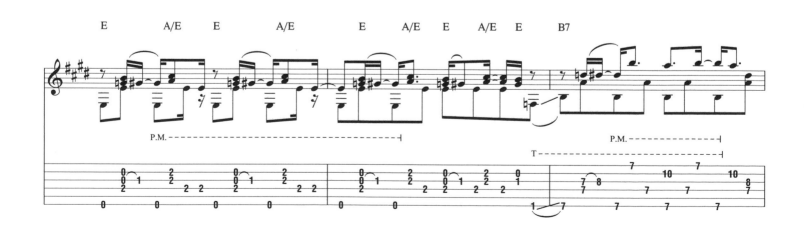

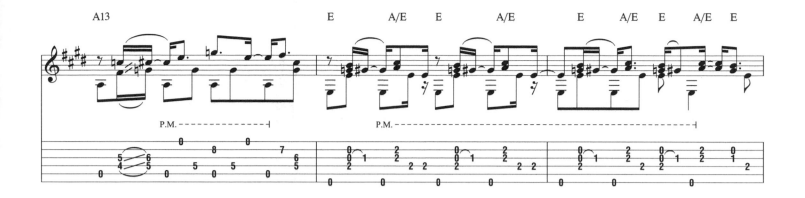

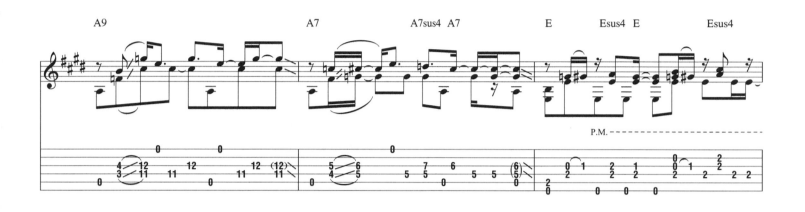

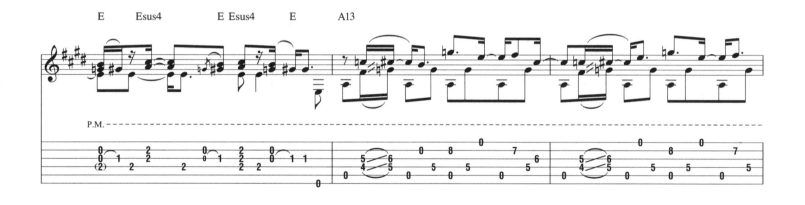

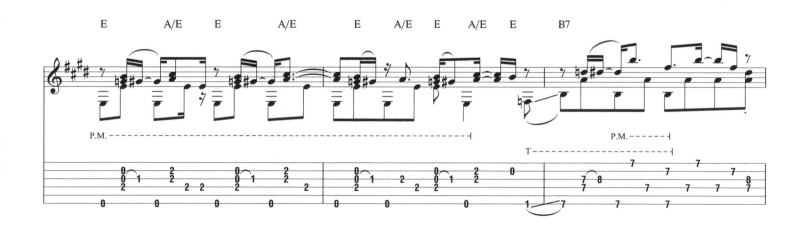

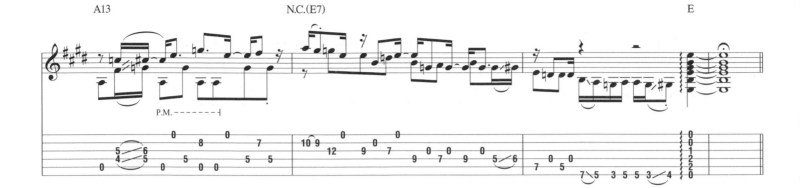

Example 43
(2:00)

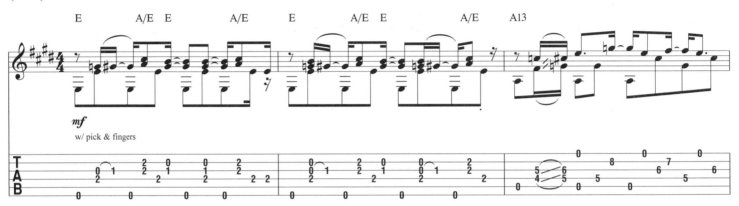

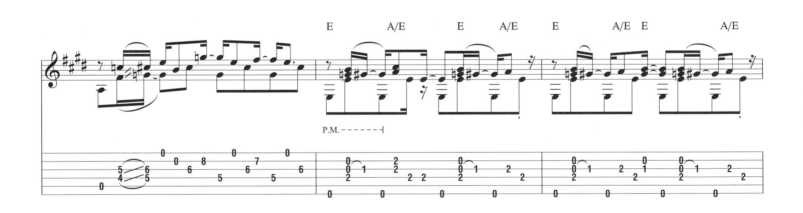

Outro and Credits

Example 44
(:50)

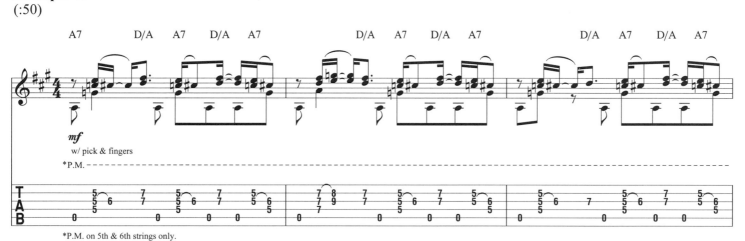

*P.M. on 5th & 6th strings only.

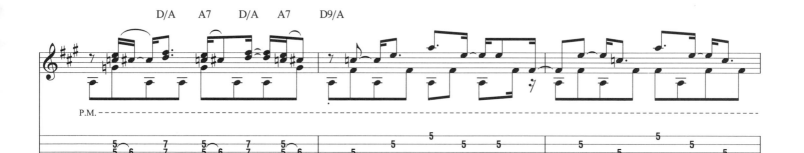

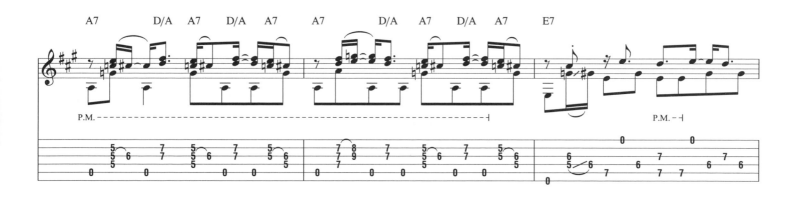

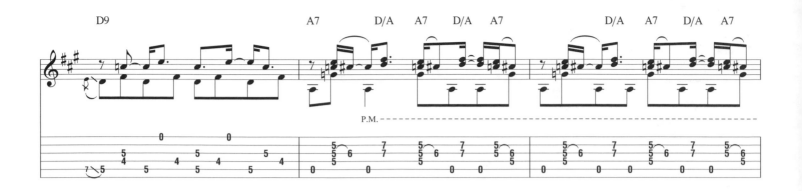

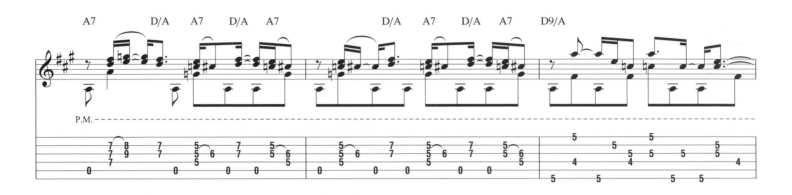

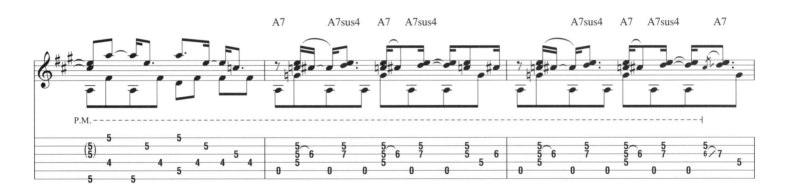

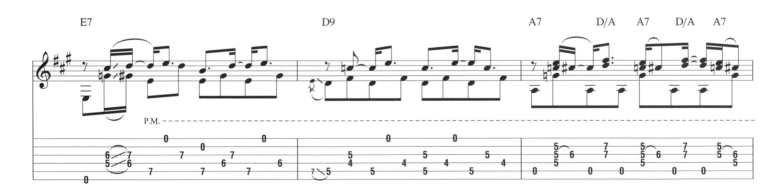

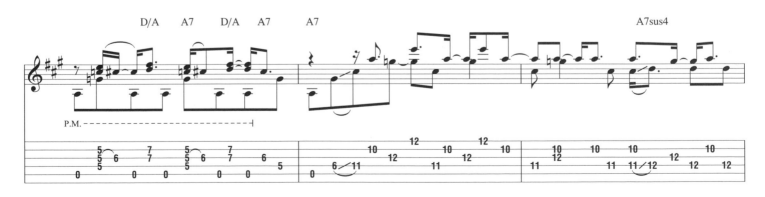

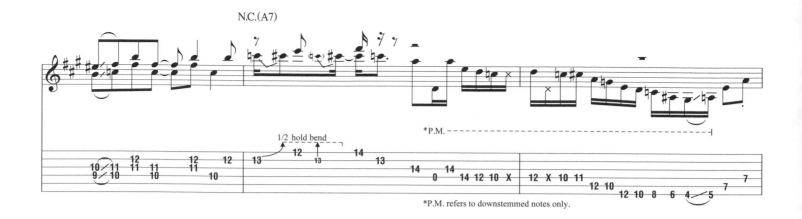

*P.M. refers to downstemmed notes only.

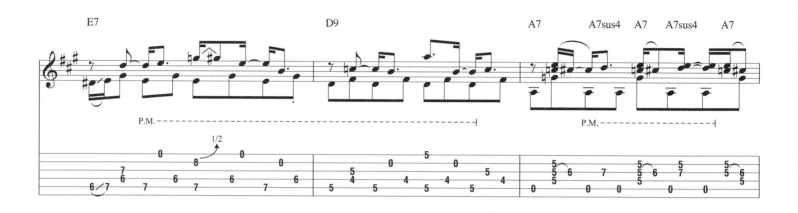

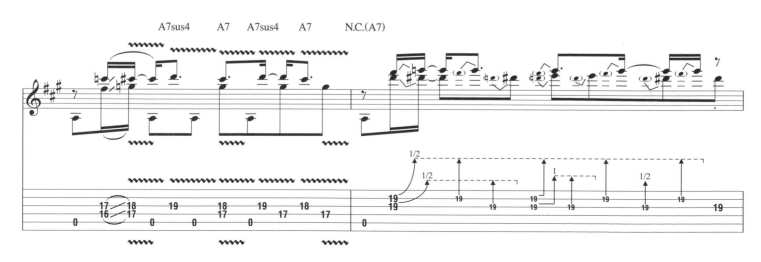

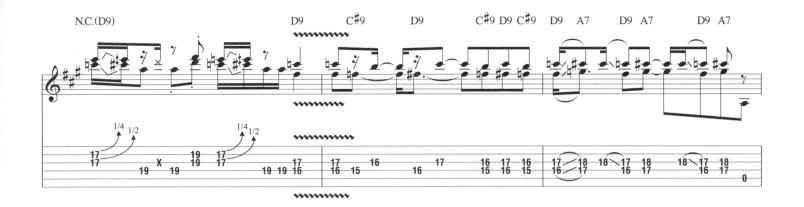

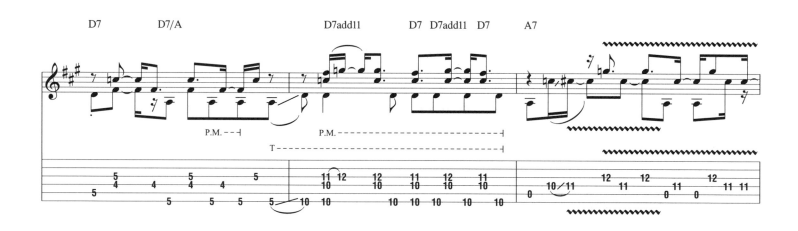

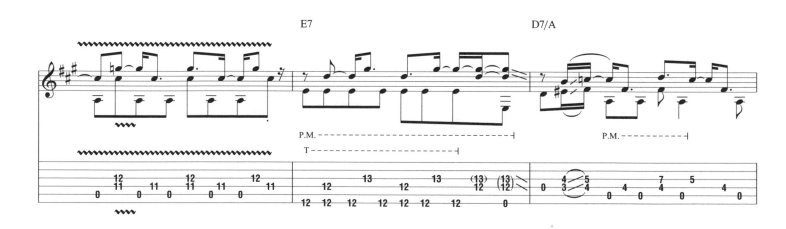

*P.M. upstemmed note.

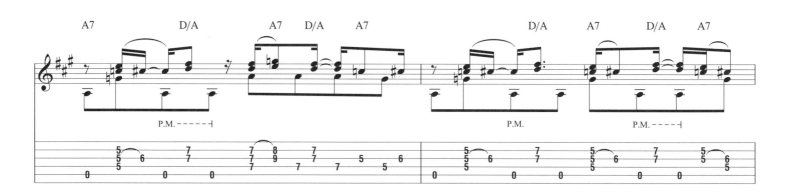

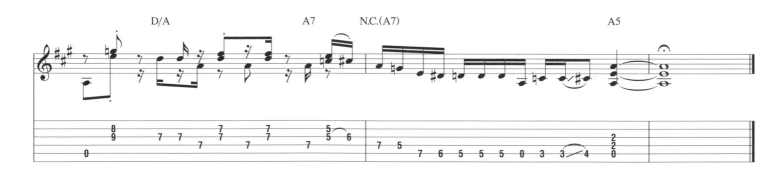

GUITAR NOTATION LEGEND

Guitar music can be notated three different ways: on a *musical staff*, in *tablature*, and in *rhythm slashes*.

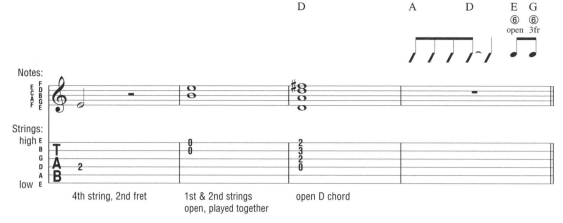

RHYTHM SLASHES are written above the staff. Strum chords in the rhythm indicated. Use the chord diagrams found at the top of the first page of the transcription for the appropriate chord voicings. Round noteheads indicate single notes.

THE MUSICAL STAFF shows pitches and rhythms and is divided by bar lines into measures. Pitches are named after the first seven letters of the alphabet.

TABLATURE graphically represents the guitar fingerboard. Each horizontal line represents a string, and each number represents a fret.

4th string, 2nd fret

1st & 2nd strings open, played together

open D chord

Definitions for Special Guitar Notation

HALF-STEP BEND: Strike the note and bend up 1/2 step.

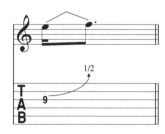

WHOLE-STEP BEND: Strike the note and bend up one step.

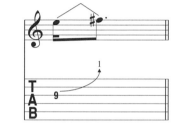

GRACE NOTE BEND: Strike the note and immediately bend up as indicated.

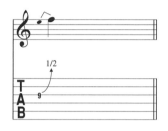

SLIGHT (MICROTONE) BEND: Strike the note and bend up 1/4 step.

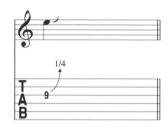

BEND AND RELEASE: Strike the note and bend up as indicated, then release back to the original note. Only the first note is struck.

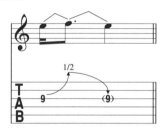

PRE-BEND: Bend the note as indicated, then strike it.

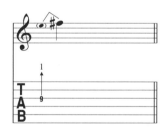

PRE-BEND AND RELEASE: Bend the note as indicated. Strike it and release the bend back to the original note.

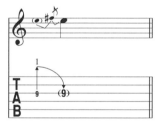

UNISON BEND: Strike the two notes simultaneously and bend the lower note up to the pitch of the higher.

VIBRATO: The string is vibrated by rapidly bending and releasing the note with the fretting hand.

WIDE VIBRATO: The pitch is varied to a greater degree by vibrating with the fretting hand.

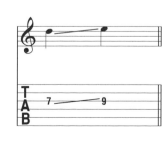

HAMMER-ON: Strike the first (lower) note with one finger, then sound the higher note (on the same string) with another finger by fretting it without picking.

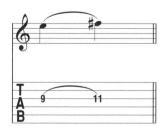

PULL-OFF: Place both fingers on the notes to be sounded. Strike the first note and without picking, pull the finger off to sound the second (lower) note.

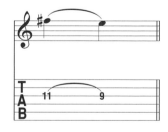

LEGATO SLIDE: Strike the first note and then slide the same fret-hand finger up or down to the second note. The second note is not struck.

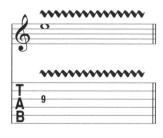

SHIFT SLIDE: Same as legato slide, except the second note is struck.

TRILL: Very rapidly alternate between the notes indicated by continuously hammering on and pulling off.

TAPPING: Hammer ("tap") the fret indicated with the pick-hand index or middle finger and pull off to the note fretted by the fret hand.

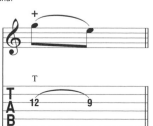

NATURAL HARMONIC: Strike the note while the fret-hand lightly touches the string directly over the fret indicated.

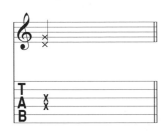

PINCH HARMONIC: The note is fretted normally and a harmonic is produced by adding the edge of the thumb or the tip of the index finger of the pick hand to the normal pick attack.

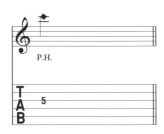

HARP HARMONIC: The note is fretted normally and a harmonic is produced by gently resting the pick hand's index finger directly above the indicated fret (in parentheses) while the pick hand's thumb or pick assists by plucking the appropriate string.

PICK SCRAPE: The edge of the pick is rubbed down (or up) the string, producing a scratchy sound.

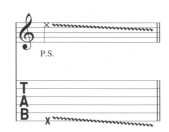

MUFFLED STRINGS: A percussive sound is produced by laying the fret hand across the string(s) without depressing, and striking them with the pick hand.

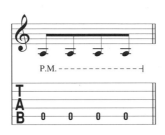

PALM MUTING: The note is partially muted by the pick hand lightly touching the string(s) just before the bridge.

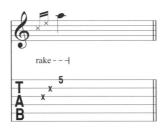

RAKE: Drag the pick across the strings indicated with a single motion.

TREMOLO PICKING: The note is picked as rapidly and continuously as possible.

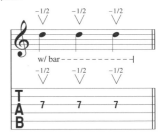

ARPEGGIATE: Play the notes of the chord indicated by quickly rolling them from bottom to top.

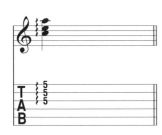

VIBRATO BAR DIVE AND RETURN: The pitch of the note or chord is dropped a specified number of steps (in rhythm), then returned to the original pitch.

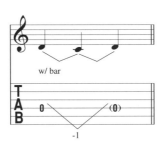

VIBRATO BAR SCOOP: Depress the bar just before striking the note, then quickly release the bar.

VIBRATO BAR DIP: Strike the note and then immediately drop a specified number of steps, then release back to the original pitch.

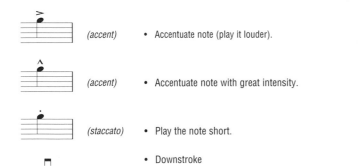

Additional Musical Definitions

(accent)	• Accentuate note (play it louder).	
(accent)	• Accentuate note with great intensity.	
(staccato)	• Play the note short.	
⊓	• Downstroke	
∨	• Upstroke	
D.S. al Coda	• Go back to the sign (𝄋), then play until the measure marked "*To Coda*," then skip to the section labelled "**Coda**."	
D.C. al Fine	• Go back to the beginning of the song and play until the measure marked "*Fine*" (end).	

Rhy. Fig. • Label used to recall a recurring accompaniment pattern (usually chordal).

Riff • Label used to recall composed, melodic lines (usually single notes) which recur.

Fill • Label used to identify a brief melodic figure which is to be inserted into the arrangement.

Rhy. Fill • A chordal version of a Fill.

tacet • Instrument is silent (drops out).

• Repeat measures between signs.

• When a repeated section has different endings, play the first ending only the first time and the second ending only the second time.

NOTE: Tablature numbers in parentheses mean:
    1. The note is being sustained over a system (note in standard notation is tied), or
    2. The note is sustained, but a new articulation (such as a hammer-on, pull-off, slide or vibrato) begins, or
    3. The note is a barely audible "ghost" note (note in standard notation is also in parentheses).